THE TILLY WOOD STORY

Some extracts from the life of a Romany Gypsy

Also some wonderful old and new photographs of the Horse Fairs she loved

Including

Appleby Fair in Westmorland
Yarm Fair near Stockton on Tees

Compiled by John McKale

Published By John Mckale

Copyright © John Mckale 2009

First published 2009

Edited by Rob Bulmer

For further information contact John
07769660194
email: info@gypsypublications.co.uk

Printed by
TEAMVALLEYPRINTERS.CO.UK

ISBN 978-0-9562266-0-0

This book is dedicated to my
beautiful twin granddaughters
Charlotte and Emily

Figure 1 Tilly Wood

Contents

Figure 2 Tilly Wood

Preface

John McKale has been around Gypsy people, and travellers for about fifty years. He has a great love for them and as a Christian Pastor has visited Gypsy families in the North of England for many years now.

John has a great interest in the Romany way of life and has many friends who are Travellers and Gypsies.

John is an ordained Minister with the Assemblies of God, Pentecostal Church.

Part of his ministry has been with Gypsy people. He knew Tilly Wood when he was a young boy attending the Newcastle upon Tyne, Town Moor Fair. There he sat around the Gypsy fires where the Gypsies assembled at the edge of the fair. This is where he met the Wood family and sat listening around the stick fires of Nation Wood and there observed Tilly and her brother Lawrence with his wife Violet who were at the fair in their open lot wagon. These Gypsies were mysterious people, with their different way of life, with their strange language, where tuvlers were cigarettes, pannie was water, gry's and juckles were horses and dogs, and yoras were eggs.

He was also fascinated by the sight of the Gypsy women and their children going out selling with their hawking baskets and bunches of elderwood flowers trying to sell them to the Gorja Rawnies.

It was also quite a sight to see the Gypsies travelling along the roads with their coloured horses pulling their ornate living wagons, and the dogs running alongside, this was a treat indeed.

Their life style was simple and uncomplicated, these people were the Gypsies. They were a different race of people, some as dark in complexion as the natives of India where they once originated from many years ago.

The old ways of the Gypsy people are fast declining, apart from at the horse fairs where you can still see the old way of life for a brief time before their holiday is over and they go back to the modern way of life.

Many of the old Gypsies are no longer with us, and this is one of the reasons why this book has been put together, so that people like Tilly Wood and thousands like her will be remembered. They were the old people who knew hardship, abuse, and rejection from the settled population.

This book will also remind us that these people were always told to move on by the law. The women often bore bite marks on their legs caused by savage dogs, as they went from door to door, trying to get a living for their families.

Tilly and others like her, have gone from us and the horse fairs such as Yarm, Appleby and Lee Gap will not be the same without them.

They lived the only life they knew, and life was sometimes hard. Life is more pleasant now for the old Gypsy people today as they are better provided for and are treated the same as everyone else, but this was not always the case.

This book was put together for your enlightenment and also so that we should thank God for life itself and not take the good things for granted.

This book is dedicated to those Gypsies and Travellers past and present, and to those who will be the future generation.

Figure 3 Tilly with John McKale, the compiler of this book

The Tilly Wood Story

Introduction

Tilly Wood was one of the most well known figures in the Gypsy and Travellers' world. She was a true Romany Gypsy and a legend in her own time - a real 'Romany Rawnie'.

These are only some excerpts, from her long and interesting life, along with some very new and old photographs of the famous Appleby and Yarm horse fairs that Tilly travelled to, and loved.

Although plagued with the infirmity of deafness, she still had a great zest for life and was greatly loved by her family, friends and acquaintances.

Tilly died in 2006 at the age of 83. This book is a tribute to her and to the only way of life she knew, and also to the many Gypsies of her generation.

Many thanks to the people who allowed me to photograph them, and to the people who loaned me their old family photographs of the Wood family. I hope this book will give folks today some idea of what it was like to be a gypsy in bye gone years.

Figure 4 Tilly Wood

Chapter 1

Early Days

The Wood family as I observed them as a young boy

I first saw the Wood family as they camped on the edge of the Town Moor Fair, Newcastle upon Tyne, around about 1955. This fair is still the largest travelling fun fair in Europe.

Figure 5 Town Moor Fair

Figure 6 Grandstand Road entrance to the fair

Figure 7 Gypsy fortune tellers at the Town Moor Fair

Figure 8 Jonas Lee and his son camped out at the Town Moor Fair in recent years

Figure 9 Town Moor Fair. The Wood family travelled in horse drawn wagons like those in the picture

Figure 10 Tina Lee at the Hoppings

When I was a lad of eleven or twelve years of age, we lived in a part of Newcastle that was situated quite near the town moor where the annual fair 'The Hoppings' was held every race week on the last full week in June.

The fair was a travelling fun fair and showmen would travel from all over England and Scotland for this major event in the showman's calendar.

This fair attracted a lot of the gypsy people, which would probably be for them the next event after the Appleby horse fair in Westmorland, which is held at the beginning of June.

At that time in the 1950's the gypsies and travellers where allowed to camp on the edge of the fair for two to three weeks, rent free. The gypsies stopped at the Grandstand Road end of the vast fair which was about a mile long. The town moor is situated about a quarter of a mile from Newcastle City Centre and runs parallel with the Great North Road which was in those days the gateway into Scotland.

What colourful people the gypsies were and along with the showmen they came from every part of the country. On the edge of the

Figure 11 The Hoppings

fairground one would meet all types of people. That's where I first saw John Eagle. John performed a strong man act using a cart wheel which he would balance on his chin. He would also swallow a brass chain and hold the last link between his teeth, before he would pull it out of his stomach to the amazement of the crowds. At that time he worked his act with his brother in law, a man called Staff, who performed as his assistant.

John Eagle and his wife Mary were there every year with their many children, John Eagle and his family lived in a small bow topped wagon. Their wagon was red in colour with a white horse painted on the bottom part of the door. Little did I know that years later John Eagle would become one of my friends, and that two of his nephews Baby Boy, and Stephen Lee who are committed Christians alongside their wives Mary and Ditty would also become very close friends to my wife and I.

Figure 12 Two old friends from many years ago. John McKale the author of this book and John Eagle

was a great privilege for me to officiate at the marriage of Stephen's lovely daughter Kerry who married Jason Lee a Staffordshire gypsy man, a few years ago.

Also on the Town Moor there were modern trailer caravans which were coming into fashion in the 1950's. In those days the horse drawn living wagons were still lived in by many of the gypsy people. But the horse drawn wagons were becoming increasingly rare. Motorisation was becoming the norm and the open lot and bow topped wagons were becoming a rarity. Travel was becoming faster and transport by lorry and trailer caravan was much quicker and more comfortable.

However, in the late 50's, a few gypsy families could still be seen travelling about in the old fashioned way, on the roads and country lanes of rural England and of course they would be seen at the fairs.

Because we lived near the fairground, it was the highlight of my year when the many hundreds of showmen with their amusements, came together to produce this large travelling fair. In those days many Gypsy families would camp on the outskirts of the fair. Those who had bought positions near the entrance did the fortune telling.

Figure 13 Newcastle Town Moor

7

I took time off school and worked on the fair, selling hot-dogs and toffee apples on a stall that belonged to Mr and Mrs Richmond. Mr Richmond was the manager on John Lings Moon Rocket speedway ride. The Richmond's had a catering stall at the side of the moon rocket ride which was managed by Mrs Richmo

I was at the fair every day, sometimes from early in the morning until late at night when I would leave at 11:00 pm to get the last bus home. To me this was the best week of my year.

As I wandered around with keen interest when the fair was being built up, I would also walk around the gypsy camp. That's where I first saw the Wood family with one open lot wagon and a milk cart which they used for transporting their water cans and bits and pieces, and also used for tatting.

John Eagle's bow top wagon was pulled next to them.

Figure 14 Lawrence and Violet Wood

I also remember seeing Mrs Wood (Nation), Tilly's mother who was certainly the matriarch of the family. There was also Lawrence, Tilly's brother with his wife Violet and their children and of course Tilly herself. Jack Wood, Tilly's dad had died by that time. Lawrence's wife, Violet, was one of the daughters of Henry and Charlotte Smith who were gypsies from the Doncaster area.

Figure 15 Henry and Charlotte Smith

One day I had the privilege of sitting around the smouldering stick fire of Nation Wood. Shortly after this it was made illegal to light fires on the fair ground because of the hazards that could be caused.

I delighted in listening to the conversations of Nation and other gypsies. They would catch up with each other's news, have general conversation and as people do, put the world to right.

Figure 16 Nation and Tilly Wood

As a naive youngster I remember saying to Nation, "The Romanies are the only true gypsies, isn't that right" to which she replied, "Yes and there are not many of us left who still live in the old way", or words to that effect. Never a truer word was spoken.

Asleep under the wagon

One morning arriving early at the fair, I passed by the Wood's wagon and was surprised to see old Nation asleep under the wagon. She was lying on heavy looking bolster and covered with blankets, a piece of canvas was wrapped around the wheels for privacy and protection. Probably Tilly and Nation used this as their bedroom. Lawrence and Violet with their children lived inside the wagon that's how some gypsy families lived in those days.

The horse that got loose

As a boy another thing stands out in my memory about Tilly - she was a woman who could handle horses. I once saw her catch a horse that had broken free from its tether. Tilly would be in her late twenties or early thirties at the time, she was a young woman with black hair and a very dark skin characteristic of the Welsh black faced gypsy people. She always wore a scarf tied around her head with her hair tucked inside. One of their horses got loose and it was Tilly who ran after it and caught it to bring it back to the gypsy camp - with her head scarf wrapped around its big neck! It was quite a sight to see this young gypsy girl leading this huge animal back home pulling it with her head scarf.

Going out Tatting

When the Wood family were camped at the Town Moor Fair, Nation and Tilly would go out with the horse and trap collecting rags and woollens. They would venture out early morning into the suburbs of Newcastle to see if they could collect peoples' unwanted clothes to take to the rag shop where they could weigh their rags and woollens in. Woollens were better value than the rags, you got more money per hundredweight.

Before they went to be weighed-in everything was sorted through to see if there were any articles of clothing that could be washed and worn. It was quite a sight to see a huge pile of clothing, curtains, shoes etc. being sorted out. Money was scarce in those post-war days and times were very hard for everyone, especially travellers. This helped to supplement their income.

Figure 17 Tilly Wood

Tilly's brother, Lawrence

Lawrence Wood was a great horse man, as was his father Jack, before him. They were real old fashioned horse dealers. Lawrence could make horseshoes as good as any blacksmith. He could practically read a horses mind. Those who used horses as a mode of transport especially gypsies needed to know much about horses and Lawrence was no exception.

The last time I saw Lawrence and his wife Violet was at a small fair in Durham City one Easter time, probably in the mid sixties. They had a stall selling children's toys and balloons.
There used to be a fair held there every Easter down by the ice rink – it's not there any more, I think it was demolished to make way for new improvements to the city.

Tilly's father Jack was a good horse dealer as well. In fact it was his own horse 'Pride' that put old Jack Wood into an early grave, after being kicked in the stomach, so Warren Coulson informed me. Warren is married to Ada, Lawrence's daughter and Jack Wood's granddaughter.

Jack Wood died when Tilly was a young girl and after his death his wife Nation and Tilly for a long time afterwards wore black clothing. Nation was left to look after the family, we will talk about that later on in the book. Jack Wood was a much loved man by his family and friends.

Figure 18 Lawrence Wood

Figure 19 Jack Wood and Nation Wood. Tilly stands looking on as her father does a deal with someone.
Young John Wood, Tilly's nephew is in the picture

"Silver Star" One of Jack Wood's Horses

Figure 21 Tilly Wood as a young girl, taken at Yarm Fair

Figure 22 Tilly Wood

Recollections of Norman Ramshaw, a well known wagon builder and painter (Ryton on Tyne)

One day I was visiting my old friend Norman and he told me that as a young lad, he and his father, who also was a man who travelled about, went to all the horse fairs in their open lot wagon. One time, it was war time Britain, they were at a fair at Darlington and were preparing to go home because of the bad weather. Norman said it had never stopped raining and he was feeling a little disappointed because of the bad weather. He told me that the fair was undercover with corrugated iron panels because of the blackout, he quotes, "Just as we were making our way home, from around the corner we saw old Lawrence Wood and his family, with the most beautiful turnout.

Figure 23 Norman Ramshaw

Figure 24 Norman Ramshaw and his wife Sylvia in their open lot

They had a good black and white horse in the shafts, pulling a handsome bow top wagon. The horse's bridle was gleaming. They looked every bit true to their race - a good looking family of Romany gypsies."

Figure 25 Norman's Dad with his Wagon

Norman remarked, "I wish I'd had a camera, what a wonderful photograph that would have been to show people who love gypsy culture and are interested in the old way of life".

Figure 26 Tilly sitting on the ground listening to a letter being read out by one of the Nicholson gypsy women

Figure 27 Isaac Nicholson at the old Birtley Site

Figure 28 The Nicholson family, who often travelled with the Woods

Chapter 2

Violet Burnside Continues The Story

Figure 29 Violet Burnside

Violet Burnside is the spitting image of her mother, Tilly.

She told me, "My mother's real name was not Tilly, but Pentcelia. She was born in the Oldham area, probably 1923 as she died in 2006 at the age of 83. Her siblings were her brothers Lawrence, Harry, and sisters Irene and Wickie".

Jack Wood, Tilley's, father was part of the Heron family. Jack's father was Aris Heron and for some reason it seems the name was changed to Wood. Tilly's mother, Nation, was a Boswell and Tilly's grandmother was also called Pentcelia and her grandfather was called Charles Boswell.

After the untimely death of Tilly's father Jack, (his grave is at Coxhoe cemetery which is a little mining village in County Durham) the family became more settled and lived in that same village Coxhoe. They bought two houses next door to each other on a street called Long Row. After these were demolished they moved to The Grove in Coxhoe and lived there until Violet was 7 years old. Violet said her mother Tilly loved Coxhoe and never wanted to leave. They were there for a little while and then moved to a house in Wingate, a village nearby.

Figure 30 Lawrence Wood stands behind his horse John Wood stands with the horses halter while one of his sisters sits on the horse

Figure 31 Nation Wood and her pet dog at Wingate

Figure 32

Figure 33 Nation Wood and Friends

17

Figure 34

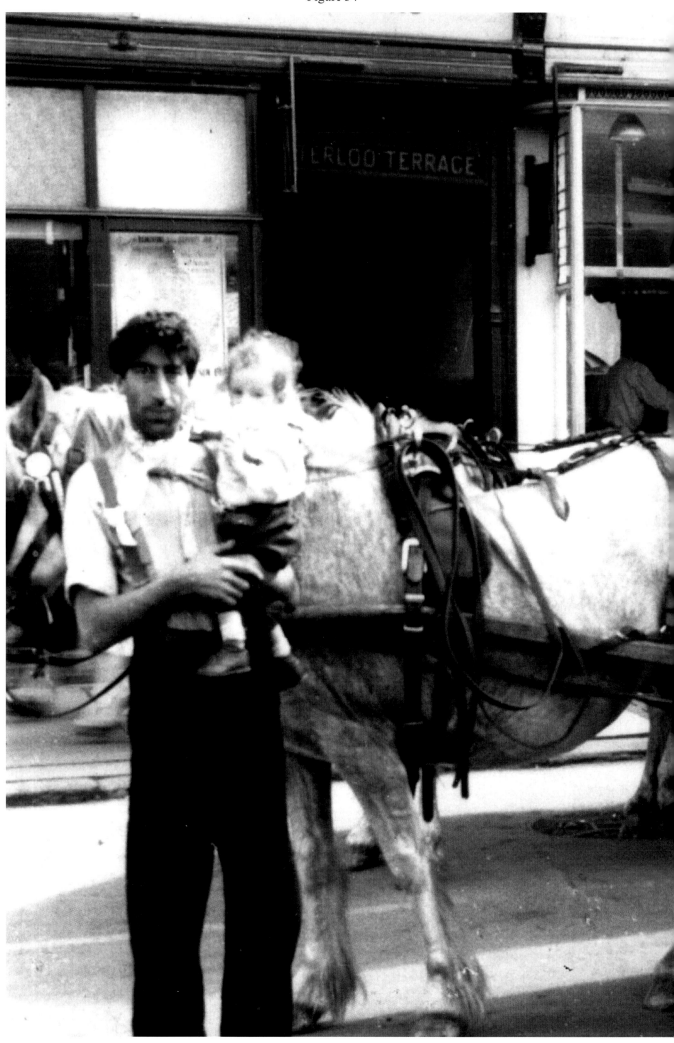

Lawrence married Violet Smith and had six children, Rodney (John), Lawrence, Carol, Linda, Logan, and Ada. Violet died when her youngest child Ada was five months old. Lawrence and his children lived with granny Nation and their two aunts Wickie and Tilly. Although they lived in a house they still travelled about to the horse fairs and from place to place in the summer.

Figure 35 Granny Nation and her grandson Logan Wood

Ten years later granny Nation died and then Lawrence, Tilly's brother died seven months after that at the age of fifty. Tilly then took on the responsibility of bringing up five of Lawrence and Violet's children single-handedly. She also had a child of her own, her daughter Violet who was about nine at that time.

Figure 37 Tilly and the children
Violet on the right

Figure 36 This is a group of gypsies. The lady with the kettle is Nation Wood, Tilly's mother, the man sitting with the mug of tea is Tilly's half brother Harry Wood

asked Violet about her earliest memories and she said they were good ones.

Figure 38 Tilly's Sister Wicky and Nation

The Woods at Wingate, County Durham

Violet recalls some facts about her early life. Tilly always slept downstairs at home on the settee. The girls slept in a room upstairs with their granny, the lads slept in another room with their father until he died.

Violet said the girls all slept in one bed with their old granny, she said they were never cold!

Every morning Tilly would get up early so that she could catch the six o' clock bus to where ever she wanted to go to sell her paper flowers that day. But before she left the house she would feed all the children. Violet goes on to say that they got hot tea and toast every morning. They didn't have a toaster so Tilly would toast the bread at the open fire. She would only do one side of the bread, put butter on it and they would enjoy the toast with their tea, before Tilly left to do her calling.

Figure 39 A very good photograph taken at Appleby. The Wood family with Tilly standing looking down with her traditional scarf tied around her head. Ada Coulson, Tilly's niece, sits on her granny Nation's knee

She went out on the dot 6:00 am every day except Sunday, with her box of paper flowers, and she always returned at six o'clock at night. The family would wait for the six o'clock bus to arrive and if she was not on it they would worry and fret, until Tilly arrived home.

Sometimes Linda, one of the girls would go out selling with her. The rest of the family had their chores to do and some went to school.

Tilly insisted that Violet went to school, and it wasn't easy in those days for a gypsy child to fit into school life. They had a different culture, and were not always accepted by the settled community.

Out selling

Tilly taught the girls how to make the paper flowers for her to sell. They were made from coloured toilet paper and fixed onto wires coated with crepe paper. They were placed in a box ready for the next day.

Figure 40 Tilly getting on in years

Each of the four girls had to make two dozen flowers every night. Tilly never came home until she had sold ninety six paper flowers every day and she did that for six days a week.

Figure 41 Tilly

illy always took with her for her food a large packet of potato crisps and that would keep her going all day.
lthough she used to often have a cup of tea at the old Eldon Square bus station café in Newcastle, or so I
·as once told by the proprietor of the cafe.

Violet recalled that when she went to school, and Tilly always insisted that she went, she would not eat school dinners - she didn't like them at all. Instead, Tilly always bought Violet a packet of Bourbon biscuits for her lunch. Tilly took pride in the fact that her daughter could read and write.

Tilly never let Violet go out hawking her flowers with her, but Linda, the oldest girl, sometimes did. Tilly often suffered a lot of verbal abuse when she went out hawking, and the children would fret if she came back late in case something had happened to her. Sometimes she would come home at night with huge dog bites on her legs, which she received when going up someone's garden path - some angry dog would try to take a bite out of her.

Figure 42 The Wood family at Appleby Fair in the 1970's

Tilly never hawked on a Sunday and she attended the local parish church and always insisted that the children did so as well and that they had their collection money too. Violet said that her God Parents were the church wardens.

Her mother bought Violet a Silver Cross pram for her dolls, which Violet loved - but that pram was also used to collect bits of coal and coke for the fire on cold winter nights!

Tilly never mixed with her Gorja neighbours, but she was well known among the gypsy community. Some of her gypsy friends were people like Nora Nicholson and Nancy Farrow.

Figure 43 Lee Gap Fair. The Wood family,
Tilly stands behind the group polishing a water can

24

Stopped by the Police

Tilly was stopped by the police one day and asked what she was doing. She was taken to the police station. They searched her and found that she was carrying a huge bag of 50 pence coins, they were some of her savings. She would not leave them at home, so every day she would carry them around with her for safe-keeping. The police asked her where she had got all the 50 pence coins from and she had a lot of explaining to do before they were finally convinced of her reasons for carrying all this money on her person instead of leaving it at home.

The Christmas party

Whenever Violet and the other girls wanted something special to wear, Tilly would say, "I know a good Gorga woman who has a daughter your age I'll try and mang (beg) some things off her.

Until they could go out and provide, for themselves, Tilly always bought the children a set of new clothes every year which had to last them.

Violet spoke about the school Christmas party. She desperately wanted a nice dress to wear. Tilly had a clothes chest in which she kept her best clothes, and things like birthday cards that she had received in years past, and receipts for any purchases she had made.

This Christmas Violet needed a new frock so Tilly went into her chest to see what she could find for Violet to wear for the party. She found one of her own dresses and gave it to Violet to wear. It was far too big and old fashioned for a young girl but Violet put it on anyway and went to the school party - only to be ridiculed and laughed at. She ended up sobbing in the toilet for the rest of the party.

The time of old Nation's death

Violet relates that when her granny Nation passed away, that she died at home with cancer. Nation would probably be in her eighties. Violet said her mother Tilly wept and wailed so loudly with grief because Tilly loved her mother so deeply.

Before she died, Nation was taken into hospital at Hartlepool. Violet fretted over her granny so much at the age of eight she decided to walk from Wingate to the hospital at Hartlepool to visit her (a distance of about nine miles!). She had no money for her bus fare home, so Nation had to borrow some money from one of the other patients for her fare.

When little Violet left the hospital instead of getting on the bus home she spent the money on sweets, and walked home back to Wingate.

Figure 44 The Wood family with granny Nation standing at the trailer door holding a baby, probably Violet. Tilly is standing with the Wood children

The rest of the family were frantic with worry not knowing what had become of her. They were out searching for her and were greatly relieved when they saw Violet walking towards them no worse for wear after her long journey.

Nation Wood died at home in Wingate and is buried alongside her husband Jack in Coxhoe Cemetery, County Durham.

Some things of interest about Tilly Wood

Tilly never really settled in a house, she never slept in a bedroom, she always longed for the travelling life, the true Romany that she was. Her natural instincts were to be out and about, she did only what she knew, what she had watched her mother and the other gypsy women do to make a living - that was to go from door to door to sell her flowers. She only used her house as a base, a place where her family lived and a place to eat and sleep.

Tilly liked beautiful things and had lots of brass ornaments and a collection of Royal Crown Derby, the gypsies favourite china which she collected over the years. Tilly never liked going to weddings or social events, she seemed to be driven by work and providing for her family.

Figure 45 Yarm Fair probably in the 1930's
This is an excellent old photograph of Gypsy life

Tilly never claimed social security benefits and even when she was eligible for her old age pension she did not claim it for a while in fear that she would not be allowed to go out and sell her flowers. She eventually claimed her pension when some official from the Social Security came and filled the forms in for her.

Although she lived in a house she never had a cooker, everything was cooked on the open fire. Pans of vegetables and potatoes and even meat were cooked this way.

Her favourite food was tripe and onions, and she always kept the cabbage water to drink, for she said it was good for the skin. Her favourite desert was baked rice pudding.

She also loved bread and butter and hot tea. Tilly was not a cook and most of the food that was cooked was done by the girls.

Sometimes broken pies and bits of food she could beg were brought into the house in those hard up days. She always did what she could to provide for her family to the best of her ability.

Violet said she never did anything for her own gain - always putting the family first. She was loved and respected by people everywhere. I myself spoke to some gypsy flower sellers at Covent Garden in London a few years ago and one of them said she knew Tilly Wood who lived up North.

She wouldn't buy herself any new clothes. Violet her daughter once bought her some sheepskin boots. Tilly thanked her for them but never wore them.

Tilly would wear two coats in the winter to keep herself warm, she was always clean and smart in the gypsy fashion, with her brightly coloured aprons, skirts and her crowning glory - her head scarf!

The man on the moon

Violet told me Tilly loved to watch the television, but was limited in her understanding, partly because she was hard of hearing and partly because she was usually too tired to watch as she had been out all day hawking her flowers.

One night she asked Violet what was on the news, Violet said there has been a man walking on the moon! Tilly didn't believe her so Violet got a slap and Tilly said in Violets own words was taking the raj. Tilly could not come to terms at that time that it was possible for someone to walk on the moon.

Paraffin to keep away the nits

Tilly would rub paraffin into all the family's hair to keep the nits away. Violet also recalls that in Tilly's later years when she helped her mother to have a bath for the first time, old Tilly 'wailed like a Banshee', saying she would die of pneumonia!

Jennifer Davies in her book 'Tales of the Old Gypsies'

Jennifer writes, "The next day I saw Aunt Tilly over the half door of her varda. The vehicle was stately, old fashioned and beautiful in green, cream and gold paint. Aunt Tilly was Mother Egypt personified, quite the darkest gypsy I have ever seen".

Tilly has gone from us, and will be missed by many for she was a colourful character who was loved by her daughter, her nieces and nephews.

Tilly has several grandchildren and great nephews and nieces who she would rightly be proud of. One of her grandsons is well educated and is training for a top engineering job in the merchant navy. The others are doing well too.

Her family loved her and they all called her 'Our Tilly'.

Tilly Wood died of old age in 2006 and is buried near her dear mother and father, her brother Lawrence and her nephew Lawrence, at Coxhoe, County Durham. Tilly has a plaque erected in her memory in the town of Yarm, near Stockton on Tees. Yarm is the horse fair which she loved a lot and visited from her earliest childhood.

Figure 46 Tilly with her granddaughter Violet-Ann

There are not very many gypsy people still alive who are like old Tilly – life was hard being a gypsy like her in post war Britain.

Poetry by Tilly's daughter, Violet Burnside

Happy Memories

Sitting round on cold dark nights

Listening to her tales by firelight
The Bourbon cream biscuits she'd give me to take
Instead of the school dinners I refused to eat
The 10p piece for sweets at the local shop
Then it was quite a lot
My hospital visits after which we'd stop
For chocolate cake and fizzy pop
"O" what a treat.
Her visits to the post office down the street
To get reduced comics she'd need
Because she knew I loved to read
The broken biscuits and broken pies she'd buy
It was the way she economised
Her faith in the Bible
When her trust was broken
To kiss it was her way of proving
That the truth was spoken
Gallons of paraffin she'd rub in our hair
The smell of which was hard to bare
No wonder I'm losing my hair
It was the way she kept the nits at bay
50p pieces saved for our Christmas club
Each one showing us her love
Packet upon packet of her favourite crisps
That always accompanied her on her hawking trips
Plain crisps only, never any other flavour
These are the memories I wish to savour

Violet Burnside

Who Was She?

I look at her picture and who do I see?
It's like looking in a mirror at a reflection of me
What are you thinking? What were you about?
I know you was my mother, though about you I knew nowt
I hear myself shout
There are so many questions spinning around in my head
Answers which will go forever unsaid
Now she's in Heaven they must stay in the past
She lies at peace now
So I must find my own peace now and hope it will last.

Violet Burnside

The Old Coloured Gry

In a meadow near the old lay bye
Stood a Gypsy boy with an old coloured Gry
As I strolled through the gate
The Gypsy boy's hatred I didn't anticipate
It so halted me in my stride
I was forced to step aside
As he came towards me
I was ready to turn and flee
Then the fear in me subsided
When I saw the grief behind it
There were no words to comfort him
So all he could say
Sorry but it's got to be this way
You know that I'm right
He's given up on the fight
He's writhing in pain
He could never be the same
His racing days are done
His end is soon to come
So as he said his goodbye
I could not help but hear him cry
As he pointed and took aim
I hung my head in shame
BANG! went the gun
The deadly deed was done.

Violet Burnside

29

Figure 47 Ada Coulson with her two sons Sanchez and Duran in 2009

Coulsons of Craghead, Co. Durham

Warren and Ada Coulson, Tilly's niece, along with their sons have a thriving business making living wagons and carts of the highest quality.

Normally John Greenwood (Yorkie) does the decorative paintwork.

Figure 48 Ada, Sanchez and Duran

Figure 49 Ada Coulson, Tilly's niece

Chapter 3

Appleby Fair

A brief history of Appleby Fair

Appleby Fair is held annually during the first week in June.

This Fair is the best known and the best loved of all the horse Fairs. It is attended by Romany families and travellers, horse dealers, and thousands of visitors, every year. They come from all over the UK to meet up with old friends and family, and of course to do business.

It is world famous and the largest of its kind in the world. It has existed as a Fair from 1685 for horse trading under the protection of a charter granted by James 11. This means that the authorities cannot cancel the Fair, although they did try quite a few years ago but Gordon Boswell (Snr) fought to keep it going.

The field on the outskirts of Appleby originally known as Gallows Hill, due to its usage as a place of execution in earlier times is now called Fair Hill and looks over the Town of Appleby.

During the Fair, horses may be found almost everywhere. They are found tethered on grass verges on the banks of the River Eden and one of the highlights of the Fair is to see them being washed in the river, then they are ready to be shown off, on the sands, or on the flashing lane near the Fair Hill.

Figure 50 Appleby Road Sign

Figure 51
The Flashing Lane

Figure 52 (Right)
Woods always stopped near the gate
where the gypsies and travellers paid
their entrance fee, for the duration of the fair

Figure 53
Two beautiful wagons on Fair Hill

Figure 54 The most beautiful gypsy wagons and carts are to be found at Appleby Fair

Figure 55 Travellers arriving at the fair looking for a place to stop

Figure 56 Tilly always took a good photograph

Figure 57 A Gypsy man at Appleby Fair.
Notice the highly decorated cart and sturdy horse

Figure 58

Figure 59

Horses being washed in the River Eden,
This is always a memorable and sometimes
a spectacular sight

Figure 60

Figure 61

Figure 62

Figure 63

Figure 64 A stopping place on the way to Appleby, on the A68 near Barnard Castle

Figure 65
Jules Lee and her family camped on Sandford Lane, waiting to pull onto Appleby Fair.
Notice the cooking arrangements; Jules was cooking bacon ribs, cabbage and new potatoes.

Figure 66

Figure 67 (Left)
Bacca and Mary Wood
Bacca was Tilly's nephew and his wife Mary was of the
Nicholson family.

Figure 68 Gypsies and travellers show off their horses and carts in the flashing lane at Appleby

Figure 69 (Left)
The Appleby Fair is an annual holiday for thousands of people, they really do enjoy the atmosphere and the meeting with old friends and family

Figure 70 (Left)
Cast iron cooking pots and kettles are still used by the more traditional gypsies. They are hung on chitty irons over the open fires. The old fashioned way of life is still maintained by many people, or at least at the horse fairs. Some travellers say that the travel to Appleby is sometimes more enjoyable than being at the fair itself

Figure 71 (Right)
The market field and the many stalls are a great attraction as part of the fair although some would not agree, they say the old fair was much better. In the photograph we see a gypsy woman selling lace table cloths.

Chapter 4

Yarm Fair

A brief history of Yarm Fair

Yarm stands on the banks of the River Tees, and was from the 12th to the 18th century the most important port on the Tees.

Yarm Fair is a tradition that stretches way back to 1214. The fair is completely different today to what it was then.

Figure 72 Road Sign of Yarm

In the past years this three day annual event which is always held on the Thursday, Friday, and Saturday of the third week of October, was once a commercial fair for the sale of cattle, horses, and cheese. It was the biggest fair in the North East of England for the sale of cheese.

Now it is a fun fair in the small high street, but gypsies and travellers horses are still run up and down the other part of the high street on Saturday morning to display those that are for sale.

The wide high street of Yarm with its Georgian facades runs through the centre of the Town. It contains shops of all varieties and also a number of pubs.

It is paved with traditional cobbles and still has a feel of yesteryear. It is on the cobbles that the gypsies and travellers park their wagons and trailers for the duration of the fair.

Tilly Wood and her family before her always came to the fair. They lived in Wingate which is a little town near Yarm

Figure 73 Gypsies camping on the High Street in 1997

Figure 74 Tilly sitting at the door of her living wagon in 1997

Figure 75 A beautiful picture of Tilly

Figure 76 (Right)
Waiting for the time to pull onto the fair,
the fair ground is the high street, the
showmen build their amusements up on
the cobbles at one end of the town and
the gypsies are on the cobbles at the other
end near the river and Yarm bridge

Figure 77
Travellers wait patiently for the time when
they can pull their wagons into town

Figure 78

Figure 79

Figure 80

Figure 81
Horses are taken to the tethering fields
before the fair starts, so the travellers
can find a good pitch quickly

Figure 82
Travellers waiting on the green verge, just outside the town for 6:00 pm,
when they can pull into the town

Figure 83

Figure 84 (Left)

Horse drawn wagons and carts are pulled into town manually, because horses will get in the way of finding a good pitch quickly

Figure 85 (Right)

Figure 86 (Left)

Figure 87 (right) Tilly's wagon arrives on a low loader, brought in by one of her nephews

Figure 88 (left) The wagon is put into position onto the cobbles. Tilly had the same spot each year near to the entrance to the town

Figure 89 (right) Here is a photograph of the late Lawrence Wood, Tilly's nephew. He relaxes after they have settled in

Figure 90 Notice in this photograph the horses are pulling not only the living wagon, but also a small trailer caravan as well

Figure 91 Different types of travelling people meet at Yarm Fair

Figure 92 Roy and Christine Morrison and their family
visit Yarm Fair with Christine's parents Blackie and Tina Lee

Figure 93 (Right)
Blackie and Tina Lee

Figure 94
More modern caravans arrive at Yarm, here we have Blackie and Tina Lee finding a place to park their trailer caravan

Figure 95 Tilly talks to an old friend

Figure 96 Lawrence and Logan Wood

Figure 97
Tilly's family - to the left of the picture are her nephews Lawrence and Logan Wood talking to their relatives

Figure 98 Tilly on the steps of her wagon at Yarm Fair

Figure 99 Harry Wood, Tilly's brother
Harry is an old gypsy who still uses a lot of the old Romany language

Figure 100 Harry Wood and his wife, Nunnie
Sadly Nunnie passed away in 2007. They were a happy Gypsy couple

Figure 101 Sometimes it's difficult taking the horses to the tethering fields,
as the traffic on Yarm High Street is busy during the day

Figure 102
Harry Wood and his friend enjoy a smoke around the fire

Stick fires are still lit and used to warm the gypsies as they have been for hundreds of years. The fires are lit on the cobble stones, alongside the main road, to the amazement of local passer bys

Figure 103 (Left)
Logan Wood and his cousin Benjie 'rokker around the yog' - chat around the fire

Figure 104 (Right) Lawrence and Logan Wood (Lawrence passed away in 2004). It is still a quaint sight to see the gypsies live as many of them used to live not so long ago, in their 'varda' living wagons

Figure 105 (Left) The Wood brothers enjoy the warmth of the open fire

Figure 106 Tilly Wood

Figure 107 Travellers enjoying a natter

Figure 108 These travelling people look tired
after a long journey

Figure 109 Ray Cooper is a well known traveller,
he always enjoys being at the horse fairs

Figure 110 Cooking is sometimes done on an open fire,
in the old fashioned way

Figure 111 These travellers enjoy each other's company.
Notice the good solid wheels on this wagon

Figure 112 Tilly loved to wear colourful clothes and her hair was always tied up
in true gypsy fashion with a colourful head scarf

Figure 113 A lovely gypsy family pose for the camera

Figure 114 Mick Darling, the well known traveller at his stall in Yarm in 1996.
He is selling pegs, sticks, and also some painted objects, water cans and also some jewellery

Figure 115 This traveller sells his goods from the bonnet of his car

Figure 116 Jonas and Angeline Lee

Figure 117 Gypsy Kathleen Lee

Figure 118 Gypsy Jules Lee and baby Jacob

Figure 119 Seasoned traveller Ted Harding

Figure 120 It's been a long journey

Figure 121 Tilly and a young friend pose for this picture

Figure 122 Gypsy children - The 'Chavvies'

The Chavvies

The Gypsies love their children and most traveller families are large. I once visited an old Gypsy woman who had over ninety grand and great grandchildren.

The old Romany words for boys and girls are chals and chies, the word for baby is tikna and the word for girl or young woman is a raklie.

In times gone bye not many Gypsy children had an education but these days they all have to attend school and this is easier for them because most Gypsies these days are settled either in houses or permanent sites.

Figure 123 Gypsy children - The 'Chavvies'

Figure 124 Gypsy children - The 'Chavvies'

Bow top and open lot wagons

The Bow-top and Open-lot horse drawn wagons were used more in the North of England than in the South. There is even a more simple type of living wagon and that is the accommodation type wagon. This is usually a cart with a simple canvas top and is used as a temporary measure, sometimes for children to sleep in or used in between times before buying a more permanent wagon.

Figure 125 (Right)

Inside the Bow-top or Open-lot wagon at the back wall is a small window which is above the bed, which always runs across the back, a mattress known as a tick is used to sleep on. It is easily stored on the bed and covered usually with a coloured silk cover.

There is usually a stove called a Queenie stove which was used in the winter to heat the wagon and to cook on when it snowed or rained.

Figure 126 (Left)

Seats were situated at the sides and cupboards were used to store crockery and other essentials. The wagon was draped with silk frills over the bed area and along the sides of the walls of the wagon.

Figure 127 (Right)

Figure 128 (Left)

The horse drawn living wagons

The living wagon was first introduced by showmen about one hundred and fifty years ago.

There were six different types made to a standard design; the Reading, the Ledge, the Bow-top, the Burton, the Showman and the Brush wagon. The first three were popular with Gypsies.

In addition to these types listed above another type came into being that is the ever popular Open-lot, which is still being built and decorated by Gypsies.

Figure 129 (Right)

They say the best type of wagon is the Bill Wright wagon. This wagon is much favoured by the travelling people, its function is elegance and easy maintenance. The body is suspended by a high under carriage with the two back wheels larger than the front ones.

Figure 130 (Left)

Figure 131 Horses are led to the grazing fields where they are well looked after, for the duration of the fair

Figure 132

Figure 133
Jim Lee and his granddaughter Angeline

Figure 134 Travelling men

Figure 136 Kathleen Lee

Figure 135 Jim, Angeline and Jonas

Figure 137 Tilly Wood